How Many Kittens Could Ride a Shark?

CREATIVE WAYS TO LOOK AT LENGTH

by Clara Cella

PEBBLE
a capstone imprint

How many **kittens** could ride a shark, thrilling the guests at the sea life park?

18
kittens!

MOO! says
the COW.
Here's a stumper:
How long is a bus,
from bumper
to bumper?

How many toy **planes**, end to end, match the wings of *this* feathered friend?

7 toy planes!

How long is
an otter?
Do you know?

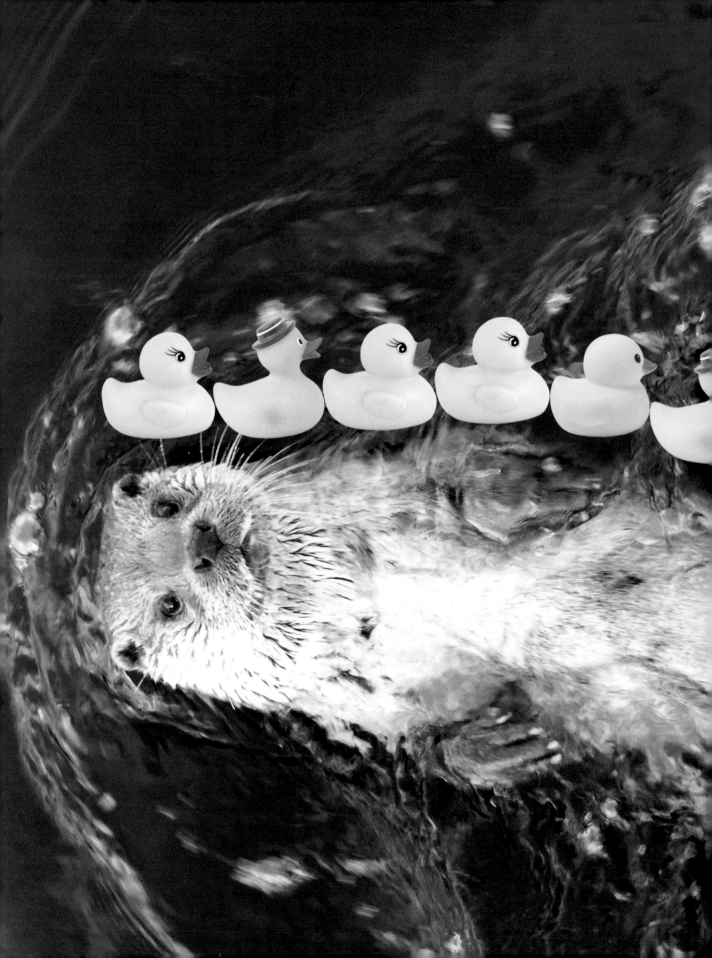

12 rubber duckies, head to toe!

Let's measure this **tail**, 1-2-3! How many gumballs would it be?

20 gumballs!

Here's an idea that sounds a bit weird: Use a **bird** to measure a beard!

This beard is 3 birds long!

Measuring a **crayon** is a piece of cake! How many inchworms would it take?

4 inchworms!

Is this statement a lie or a truth? A mouse is as long as a lion's tooth.

TRUTH!

LOOK FOR OTHER BOOKS IN THE SERIES:

Pebble Sprout is published by Pebble, an imprint of Capstone.
1710 Roe Crest Drive, North Mankato, Minnesota 56003
www.capstonepub.com

Library of Congress Cataloging-in-Publication Data is available on the Library of Congress website.
ISBN 978-1-9771-1323-8 (library binding)
ISBN 978-1-9771-2010-6 (paperback)
ISBN 978-1-9771-1327-6 (eBook PDF)
Summary: Introduce pre-readers to the math concept of length with eight goofy, non-standard measuring units, including kittens, toy airplanes, and gumballs. Delightful composite photos and a sprinkling of text illustrate the length of a shark, a lemur tail, a crayon, and more.

Image Credits

Shutterstock: 5 Second Studio, 4 (gray kitten), 5, almond, 20–21 (lemur), Anest, 28 (stretched inchworm), 29, Anna Utekhina, cover (cat's paws), 1, Charles Brutlag, 23, 24 (finch), 25 (finches), CLS Digital Arts, 29 (inchworm), ConstantinosZ, 12 (red, white, and blue toy plane), cynoclub, 4 (Bengal kitten), 5, Dmitry Kalinovsky, 4 (dark orange tabby kitten), 5, Dx09, 9 (front left), Eric Isselee, 3, 8 (front left and right), 9 (front right), 11, 30, 31 (mouse), Ewa Studio, 4 (orange tabby kitten), 5, GrashAlex, 12 (red toy plane), 13, GrigoryL, 4 (striped kitten), 5, Jay Bo, 31 (lion), Kitch Bain, 20 (gumballs), 21, Luis_Vazquez, 28–29 (crayons), Lukas Walter, 4–5 (shark), M Kunz, 7, Mtsaride, 27, Nerthuz, cover (top), back cover, Picsfive, 16 (rubber duck with eyelashes), 17, Randy van Domselaar, 15, ReaLiia, 12 (blue toy plane), 13, Sebastian Reinholdtsen, 16–17 (otter), sebra, 24–25 (bearded face), Sergey Uryadnikov, 12–13 (eagle), silky, 8–9 (bus), Sittirak Jadlit, 16 (plain rubber duck), 17, Tony Campbell, 4 (white and gray tabby kittens), 5, tratong, 19, Tsekhmister, 16 (rubber duck with blue hat), 17, Yuliia Sonsedska, cover (cat), 1

Editorial Credits

Editor: Jill Kalz; Designer: Ted Williams; Media Researcher: Svetlana Zhurkin; Production Specialist: Katy LaVigne

Printed and bound in the USA.
PA99